Scottish Steam

44703

Scottish Steam

W. J. Verden Anderson

A Tribute by

Keith Verden Anderson & Brian Stephenson

This book is dedicated to:

My mother, Birgitta, brother and sisters, Katrina, Graeme, Anna, Veronica and Susie for whom the spirit of Dad lives on in us.

Niamh and Mickey for giving us the time and encouragement to fulfil our ambition of making this book.

Page 1: Great North of Scotland Railway Class D40 4-4-0 No 62277 *Gordon Highlander* takes water at Craigellachie before taking the Speyside train to Boat of Garten, c1951.

Frontispiece: Stanier 'Black Five' 4-6-0 No 44703 slows for its stop at Gleneagles with an evening Glasgow Buchanan Street–Dundee West train in 1964. The Ochil Hills lie behind the train, with a cleft in them that is Glen Eagles itself.

Left: Peppercorn Class K1 2-6-0 No 62034 battles with the gradients on the Mallaig line with a train from Fort William.

Right: Thompson LNER Class A2/1 4-6-2 No 60507 *Highland Chieftain* with a northbound fitted freight near Granthouse on 11 April 1954.

First published 2004

ISBN 0 7110 2992 X

Published by Ian Allan Publishing

an imprint of Ian Allan Publishing Ltd, Hersham, Surrey KT12 4RG.
Printed by Ian Allan Printing Ltd, Hersham, Surrey KT12 4RG.

Code: 0403/B2

Preface

'Life is like a journey to an object as elusive as the crock of gold under the rainbow's end; the trick is to enjoy the journey with all its ups and downs, enjoy the view from the window be it fine scenery or even ugly back streets, give and receive the best out of the other passengers.'

Looking through the pages of *Trains Illustrated* in the late 1950s and early 1960s, one often comes across glorious photographs of steam at work in Scotland, and these were of such a high standard of composition that you knew long before reading the caption credit that they were taken by W. J. V. Anderson.

'Bill', as he was known to all, also co-edited *Steam in Scotland* Volumes 1 and 2, with Derek Cross, which were published in 1968 and 1972. Bill always intended to publish 'another book' one day but was prevented from doing so by his untimely death in 1989, at only 57 years old. It is therefore with great honour that this intention can now be realised by his dear friend, Brian Stephenson, and his youngest son, Keith.

We are proud to present this album of Bill's Scottish steam photos taken from 1950 to 1967, which features classic WJVA black-and-white photography and Bill's colour work, which has rarely seen the light of day.

We hope you enjoy this book as much as we have enjoyed compiling it.

Keith Verden Anderson
Brian Stephenson

60152

Introduction

'The sun shone intermittently through the gaps in the clouds of the grey September sky and glinted on the waves of the Eden estuary. A few seagulls wheeled angrily around the foreshore, their cries completely drowned out by the cause of the disturbance. The air was alive with the noise of aeroplanes — of Tiger Moths, Hawker Harts and other long-forgotten bi-planes — for on this day in the late Thirties the gates of RAF Leuchars had been opened to the public, and they were showing their paces.

'The air displays of prewar days were much more immediately impressive than the all-too-fast rumble and bang of today's machines. The bi-planes flew in tight formation, doing fantastic aerobatics, all in front of your noses. The climax of the day was always a battle, with an attack on a mock fort on the other side of the airfield, which involved much smoke, flame and noise. On this particular afternoon, just as the climax of the show was reached, a small boy of six or seven clutched his mother's hand and excitedly pointed across the airfield, and was heard to exclaim, "Look mummy — there's a train!"

'It was probably a 'Glen' class 4-4-0 on the line between St Andrews and Dundee. She must have made a pretty picture running along the seashore with the low hills of East Fife in the background. The small boy, who had managed to get his values in the right order, forgot the incident, but a seed had been planted, though it was to remain dormant for a number of years.

Peppercorn Class A1 4-6-2 No 60152 *Holyrood* heads an evening car sleeper train for the south away from Perth near Bridge of Earn in summer 1963

'Other early encounters with trains were on family camping holidays, four miles north of Blair Atholl at the Falls of Bruar. This location coincided with the lower section of the severe 15-mile climb of Druimuachdar Summit, on the Highland line between Perth and Inverness. This climb, significant more for its length rather than its steepness, starts in the picturesque, well-wooded village of Blair Atholl and follows the valley of the river Garry to its bleak watershed with the Truim. The climb was always a severe test for locomotives, and until the late 1950s the heavier trains were all banked.

'The family camped between the railway and the river, and I well remember lifting the back of the tent to watch in awe as the trains climbed past. The train engines always seemed to be working hardest, and the banking engines at that time looked to me to be struggling just to keep up, panting along like faithful dogs, rather than actually pushing the train.

'My first journey up the bank properly was on the way to family summer holidays on Speyside during the war. I recall the happy camaraderie of the overloaded, overcrowded trains of the period. At Blair Atholl most passengers got out for a much-needed stretch. There was a distinct atmosphere of preparation for the assault on the bank. The train engines, a pair of Class 5s, were watered and checked over by their drivers.

'There would then be a false start, causing considerable anxiety to the uninitiated, who thought they were being left behind. It was, of course, merely to bring the rear of the train into the platform and clear the crossing point to enable the banker, which had been waiting on the up road, to buff to the rear. This was the signal for the promenaders to remount. The guard's whistle blew, insignificant amongst the hoosh of safety valves; there would be a crowning exchange between the LMS hooters on the two engines at the front and the cheekier Caley hooter on the banker, all this to ensure that they started in unison. Off we went, with the smell of coal smoke mingling with that of pines and heather, drifting in through the windows from the warm afternoon. These things were all part of the holiday.'

The 'small boy of six or seven' was Bill. These earliest recollections of Bill's encounters with steam engines came from notes hand-written by him, which were found in his darkroom.

Bill was born in Edinburgh on 28 March 1932, the eldest son of Eric Verden Anderson, senior partner in the family paper-making business of Smith,

A photograph taken from the long footbridge just north of Rugby station, showing 'Rebuilt Royal Scot' No 46138 *The London Irish Rifleman* approaching with an up express as Fowler 'Jinty' No 47379 shunts in the background.

Anderson & Co of Leslie, in Fife. He was raised at Leslie in the family house overlooking the Fettykil Paper Mill in the valley below, where he would have been able to gaze down on the daily goods train from Markinch. Usually a 'J37', the locomotive shunted coal and finished goods wagons in the paper mill's sidings — although Bill never mentioned that this nurtured his interest in railways. He often likened the paper-making machines to steam locomotives, for they conveyed to him a similar impression of speed and graceful works of mechanical art, although on an even grander scale.

Bill recalled how his interest developed …

'The trouble really started when I was sent to school in Rugby in 1946. Possibly it was part out of homesickness for far-off Scotland, but an assignment was made with another boy at the back of the maths class to accompany him to watch trains that afternoon. What better place could there have been than Rugby at that time? We sat on the bank about 1/4 mile south of the station, in the shadow of the Great Central viaduct. The Great Central itself provided an endless succession of coal trains bound for the capital behind Robinson 2-8-0s and, of course, No 6166 Earl Haig *as sure as clockwork every day on the same southbound local. That was only the bonus. The main attraction was the LMS West Coast main line, with the busy Rugby shed in the background.*

'I can still see the rocking and rolling antics of the locomotives as they took the points where the through lines rejoined the lines which came from the station. There would be a fleeting glimpse of white knuckle from the fireman's hand on the cab side. A large, angry dollop of white water would splash down from the back of the tender, which had just been freshly filled on the Rugby troughs. The driver, clutching the regulator, as soon as the engine settled down would yank it open, and the engine, usually a 'Scot' or a 'Jubilee', would stutter into a magnificent three-cylinder roar that would echo back off the surrounding buildings as it climbed out to Hillmorton and the Kilsby Tunnel.

'The coaches were left to look after themselves; none of this present-day business of the whole train clearing the slack. The roll, of course, was its own progenitor, as the water made the track very spongy at this point. This was in the years just after the war, when maintenance on both track and locomotives was at a very low ebb. Obviously the drivers were very skilful. Without speedometers, they knew exactly how far they could push their luck in the struggle to save vital seconds.

'Before long I was hooked, but I quickly saw the futility of just watching trains. However fascinating the scene was, it was a passing one in more senses than one, and a camera was essential. Looking back, I never imagined that it would pass so quickly, but I suppose that is a commentary on life itself.

'It was not long, therefore, before the inevitable box camera was taken along on excursions to the side of the railway. Surprisingly few photographs were taken in those early years, as film was extremely difficult to obtain. A small schoolboy, in a strange town, could only do this by persistently badgering the various suppliers. Each exposure had to count — a factor which probably affected my attitude to photography for a great many years.

'Before I left school I had graduated to a more effective folding camera, a Voigtlander Bessa with a less than perfect Voigtar lens, bought second-hand for £10 — an enormous sum in those days. Film had become more plentiful, but I had witnessed an ominous event — the first run of the pioneer LMS diesel express engines. The significance of this escaped us completely. The new machines were untried and temperamental; it was inconceivable that they would replace steam in such a short time.'

Bill and school friend Simon Reid with A. W. V. Mace, their science master and an accomplished railway photographer, stand beside ex-SR Bulleid 'Merchant Navy' No 35005 *Canadian Pacific* at Rugby shed in February 1950, when the locomotive was visiting the Rugby Test Plant.

During his National Service in the RAF Bill had the good fortune to be posted to RAF Kinloss for some of the time, and this gave him the opportunity to explore the Great North of Scotland lines, on his bike, as well as the local Highland line to Inverness. Many unique photographs were taken. When he returned to his home he took photographs on the main line north from Edinburgh to Dundee, where it passed near Leslie on the climb from Markinch to Lochmuir going north, from Ladybank coming south and also around Thornton Junction.

By this time Bill was developing his technique — and had in fact seen his first photographs published in *Trains Illustrated* while still at Rugby school in 1950 — but was finding the old Voigtlander less than perfect. The focus was uneven, the corners of the negatives faded away (which makes them the very devil to print today), and the shutter release was such that it was very easy to spoil the photograph as a result of camera shake. So in the spring of 1954 Bill invested in a 2½in x 3½in plate camera — which was to serve him for the next 10 years — and with this he produced some of the finest pictures ever taken on Scotland's railways.

The improvement in Bill's photography was immediate, and one of the first pictures taken with the new camera — depicting ex-GNSR 'D40' 4-4-0 No 62267 leaving Craigellachie — won the 1954 *Trains Illustrated* photographic competition!

In 10 years Bill produced approximately 1,800 photographs using glass plates — not a large number, but they were to a very high standard that numerous people tried to emulate. Bill's recollection of the plate camera was not altogether positive ...

'The plate camera was, quite frankly, totally unsuited to the job. It was clumsy, slow to use and difficult to hold. Furthermore, some of the plate-holders were not reliable when it came to keeping the light out. For all that, though, the camera was one which made you take good pictures. It made you spend a long time planning each shot. It seems strange to think that I used to go out to a busy place like Beattock for a day's photography with just six reliable plate-holders.'

Most of the photographs Bill took with the plate camera depicted Scotland or the railways around Shap. He generally did not take photographs with this camera unless the light was good and the subject matter suitable, in terms either of cleanliness or of how the exhaust was behaving. A notable exception with the wind blowing in the wrong direction was the unusual sight of a '4F' 0-6-0 leaving Crianlarich with a freight for Oban in April 1955. This engine was going so slowly that Bill managed to take several shots on foot — even with the problems of changing plates!

'There was no question of photographers chasing trains then. We simply stood in a suitable place waiting for one to come to us. Moreover, we could afford to be choosy, waiting for clean engines or those from classes we particularly liked. A dirty Class 5 was not photographed unless the location was outstanding.'

On finishing his national service in the RAF, Bill joined the family firm and learned the technical side of paper-making, becoming greatly respected by the trade for his expertise and ultimately ending up as Chairman, upon the death of his father. After work in the paper mill, Bill would often dash out on summer evenings to photograph the 4.15pm Edinburgh Waverley–Aberdeen train climbing the nearby bank from Markinch to Lochmuir, usually with an 'A4', or would go over to the gently rising grades between Mawcarse Junction and Glenfarg, with the mountainous 'Paps of Fife' in the background, to see the 4.05pm Edinburgh Waverley–Perth — again, often 'A4'-hauled. This would be followed by the 4.37pm Glasgow Queen Street–Perth, usually headed by a 'Director', 'Scott' or 'Glen', or on occasions a 'Caley' Class 3P 4-4-0. In later years he would head for the Perth–Glasgow line to capture the famous 4.45pm fish train to the south. At holiday times he would head for the Highlands, West Highlands or the Callander and Oban lines.

Bill's love of the Scottish landscape is self-evident from his photographs and in particular the way he would use specimen trees to enhance his pictures. He also loved hill-walking, camping and skiing. The train was in many respects the icing on the cake in completing the image that he tried to capture. He was a perfectionist, always trying to capture the ultimate portrait, which explains why he returned to his favourite spots time after time. Where necessary he would undertake a 'spot of gardening' to ensure that no stray branches would be in the photograph.

This photograph clearly demonstrates Bill's artistry with a camera. Gresley 'J38' 0-6-0 No 65901 is setting wagons, loaded with coal for the mill boilers, back into the Smith, Anderson & Co Fettykil paper-mill siding at Leslie in April 1965. Note the trees framing the picture and all the other elements that go to make this scene so interesting. Bill would have been the first to admit that luck played a great part in pictures like this, but it was his ability to see the possibilities before they happened that counted; so many of us see the picture when it is too late to do anything about it. The photograph was taken with the 6x7cm Linhof camera using Kodak Tri-X film.

Towards the end of 1963 Bill Anderson decided to retire his trusty plate camera in favour of a Linhof '6x7' press camera, which used 120-roll film. Derek Cross had been using a similar camera for some years, and this probably prompted Bill to purchase it — but it was somewhat over-engineered and proved unreliable. However, in the final five years of BR steam traction Bill produced around 800 black-and-white photographs with the Linhof. Being able to use roll film, he indulged in a small amount of colour-transparency work. By this stage he also had a 35mm Minolta camera, and with this he experimented with colour film, much of which is seen in this book. He also experimented with shots of moving trains using an electronic flash on the 35mm camera — probably much to the consternation of passing locomotive crews!

The colour film was slow and difficult to use in the early days, and with black-and-white film being at its best, the latter was preferred. Many of Bill's earlier colour slides deteriorated badly, Kodachrome 25 being the exception. Luckily he switched to this film when it was introduced in 1961, replacing the very slow 8ASA Kodachrome, and found that it maintained its colour fastness well.

Above: Enjoying an ice cream, Bill's eldest son Graeme watches Stanier 'Black Five' No 45136, which has just arrived at Perth General station with the 2.10pm fish train from Aberdeen in August 1963. This train continued its journey south at 4.45pm behind 'Britannia' Pacific No 70044.

Left: One of the night-time flash photographs showing 'A2' Pacific No 60527 *Sun Chariot* heading out of Perth with the 'Up Special TPO' early in 1964. Note the electronic flash has frozen the locomotive but how the lights have moved during the exposure.

Unfortunately, as the colour films improved, the changing railway scene was fast deteriorating, with the locomotives becoming less well looked-after in their latter years. Looking through the slides, one can almost see the panic that was setting in right at the end. Bill took photographs of the final steam-hauled services even with the engines being filthy or the weather less than perfect. Time was running out, and the next slide in the box would invariably capture the day that the train appeared with a gleaming pair of brand-new Type 2 diesels. That would be the last time Bill visited that location.

As the steam-worked lines gradually decreased in number in Scotland, Bill began to travel further afield, visiting railways around North and South Blyth and Consett, where the dirty industrial scenes were a stark contrast to the fresh heather-clad mountain passes of Scotland. He also made a first visit with his camera to the Settle & Carlisle line, camping by the lineside with his eldest son, Graeme. The last of the traditional 'Anderson' lines was the Killin branch, which Bill visited several times towards the end of its existence in 1965.

Left: On a rare visit to Ayrshire, Bill photographed Class 4F 0-6-0 No 44325 approaching Monckton, between Troon and Prestwick, with a southbound ballast train as Birgitta, his fiancée, watched in July 1955. This photograph was taken with the Newman & Guardia plate camera on the 6x9cm Ilford HP3 plate.

After steam ended in Scotland, and due to increasing commitment to business and family, railway photography for Bill mainly became a holiday occupation, but it was nonetheless influenced by a chance meeting on Shap Fell when he was out with Derek Cross in 1964. They were sheltering behind a dry-stone wall from the ever-present wind when over the wall came the renowned Swiss photographer Harald Navé, who, after exchanging greetings, went on his way. Little did Bill know then that he was to meet Harald again by chance the following February when he was taking a skiing holiday at Davos — and a special train was running hauled by one of the Rhaetian Railway 2-8-0s. After this meeting they became firm friends and made several overseas trips together.

The Linhof lasted until 1972, when Bill seized upon one of the then brand-new Pentax '6x7' cameras — which he immediately pronounced as the best camera ever made for railway photography. He was almost certainly the first railway photographer to use one of these now relatively common cameras.

While steam lasted in Europe, Bill also visited Austria, France, Finland, Germany and Spain and went on to photograph steam in South Africa, South America and India, in addition to further visits to Norway and Sweden for some of the museum lines.

In latter years, together with his wife Birgitta, he purchased a derelict water mill near Balquhidder and set about restoring it as a family holiday home for his growing family, which grew to six — Katrina, Graeme, Anna, Veronica, Susie and Keith — even to the extent of getting the water wheel turning once again. During the 1980s he became more active in the UK, photographing preserved lines and, increasingly, the contemporary BR scene in Scotland. It was during this time that Keith spent many happy hours out with his father in the last years of his life photographing diesels on the Highland lines and elsewhere.

With Bill's death on 23 September 1989 at the early age of 57 after a characteristically courageous three-year fight against cancer, Scotland lost the finest railway photographer it is ever likely to know. Brian lost a railway-photographer friend who, in his modest way, set an example to all who took up this rewarding hobby.

'For, like so many other things, the giants of steam have gone forever, except for the few which will sleep out their years in museums and in preservation. Photography can only catch a glimpse of what the real days of steam were all about, with the busy main-line junctions with steam blowing about on all sides.

'Apart from the pictures he takes, the photographer always remembers 'the one that got away', for they often leave the more vivid impression. I will never forget my first sight of a pair of 'K2s' leaving Bridge of Orchy station on the morning train from Fort William to Glasgow. One of them is still in wartime black. The other has a fresh coat of LNER apple green. As they struggle away from the station, the wind catches the copious quantities of smoke and steam and whirls them up the slopes of the mountains, whose tops are still snow-clad. We can only carry these pictures in our imagination, and they will always be better than the pictures that we managed to take.'

Keith Verden Anderson
Brian Stephenson

Edinburgh and the East Coast Main Line

Right: With the superb backdrop of the former North British Hotel, Gresley LNER Class A3 4-6-2 No 60090 *Grand Parade* departs from Edinburgh's Waverley station at 1.30pm with the southbound 'Heart of Midlothian' for London King's Cross *c*1958/9. This express conveyed through carriages from Aberdeen, departing at 9.40am and arrival at King's Cross was after 9pm. This Pacific, from Haymarket shed, had recently (August 1958) been fitted with a double chimney. Having entered service in August 1928, the original *Grand Parade*, named after the 1919 Derby winner, was replaced by a new engine after being involved in the Castlecary accident in 1938.

60142
52
A

Left: Peppercorn Class A1 4-6-2 No 60142 *Edward Fletcher* bursts from Penmanshiel Tunnel at the summit of the 1-in-96 climb from Cockburnspath with a southbound express from Edinburgh Waverley on 11 August 1954. Part of this tunnel collapsed during work to lower the track for electrification and the line had to be re-routed around the blockage.

Upper right: Later the same day, in glorious evening light, Gresley Class K3 2-6-0 No 61901 from Tweedmouth shed heads north with a fitted freight train composed of meat vans returning to Aberdeen along the coast just over the border into Scotland between Berwick-upon-Tweed and Burnmouth.

Lower right: A grimy Peppercorn Class A1 Pacific — No 60143 *Sir Walter Scott* from Gateshead shed — accelerates after slowing for the curve through Dunbar with the southbound 'Flying Scotsman' — the 10am Edinburgh Waverley–King's Cross — in November 1959.

Above: On the first day that Bill Anderson had his 35mm Minolta camera, former North British Railway Class J35 0-6-0 No 64533 heads away from the East Coast main line at Portobello East Junction with a freight train for Niddrie Yard in March 1961. The ECML can just be seen in the right-hand background, while Portobello power station is in the centre. The driver of Gresley LNER Class V2 2-6-2 No 60868 is phoning the signalbox, seeking permission to proceed back to St Margaret's shed.

Right: A cheerful scene at Craigentinny as the driver of double-chimney Class A3 4-6-2 No 60093 *Coronach,* nearing the end of its journey with a Carlisle–Edinburgh Waverley express, exchanges greetings with the driver of Thompson Class B1 4-6-0 No 61007 *Klipspringer*, waiting to leave the carriage sidings with empty stock for Waverley in August 1959. This was one of the four 'A3' Pacifics allocated to Carlisle Canal shed, which were seldom seen away from the Waverley route.

60093
61007

60152
PORTOBELLO EAST
20

Left: This photograph — regarded by Bill as his first decent colour slide — was also taken on the first day he had the Minolta camera. Class A1 4-6-2 No 60152 *Holyrood* passes under the elevated signalbox at Portobello East Junction with the southbound 'Queen of Scots' Pullman — the 11am from Glasgow Queen Street to King's Cross — in March 1961. One of the former Waverley pilots, Class J83 No 68477, waits patiently in the background.

Upper right: Gresley LNER Class K3 2-6-0 No 61969 from Heaton shed gets the road from Meadows Junction with a long train of empty mineral wagons that will soon join the East Coast main line on that same day in March 1961.

Lower right: Nicely turned-out Gresley LNER Class V3 2-6-2T No 67620 from St Margaret's shed has just passed Craigentinny carriage sidings (just beyond the bridge) on a local trip working from Portobello and heads towards Edinburgh Waverley in October 1961.

Left: A scene at the former Caledonian Railway Princes Street terminus in Edinburgh, showing Stanier LMS Class 5 4-6-0 No 44786 departing in the late evening as another member of the class replenishes its tender with water by the signalbox *c*1962. This station closed in September 1965, when its remaining services were transferred to the former NBR Waverley station.

Above left: BR Standard 'Clan' Pacific No 72002 *Clan Campbell* departs from Edinburgh Princes Street with the 1.30pm train for Glasgow Central on 14 May 1956. This was one of Bill's earliest colour slides taken on 8ASA Kodachrome film. Note the camera bag left carelessly on the platform. The engine carries the wrong setting of the 'Caley' route indicator, which should be set as an 'L'.

Above right: Later the same day, Fairburn LMS Class 4MT 2-6-4T No 42162 departs from Princes Street with a late-afternoon local for Carstairs. This engine was allocated to Edinburgh's former Caledonian Railway shed at Dalry Road, which provided motive power for the local passenger and goods trains on the routes west from the city to Carstairs and Glasgow Central.

Fife

Left: One of the celebrated Gresley LNER Class K4 2-6-0s built for the West Highland line, No 61996 *Lord of the Isles* enters North Queensferry station from the short tunnel at the summit of the 1-in-70 climb from Inverkeithing to the Forth Bridge with the Saturday-only 12.45pm stopping train from Markinch to Edinburgh Waverley in October 1959. The five engines in this class were at Thornton Junction shed only from May (two) and October (three) 1959 until withdrawn in October-December 1961.

Right: Fitted with German-style trough-type smoke-deflectors, Class A3 Pacific No 60100 *Spearmint* leaves the Forth Bridge at North Queensferry with a Millerhill–Dundee fitted freight in spring 1965 — shortly before it was condemned at Darlington Works, in June 1965.

29
60100

60537

Left: Peppercorn LNER Class A2 4-6-2 No 60537 *Bachelors Button* starts the 1-in-70 climb from Inverkeithing to the Forth Bridge with a Dundee Tay Bridge–Edinburgh Waverley semi-fast in spring 1962. Practically all the trains on the lines from Perth and Dundee to Edinburgh were rostered for diesel traction by this date, so the Pacific was most likely deputising for a failure.

Right: On a frosty morning in November 1966 Gresley LNER Class J38 0-6-0 No 65915 leaves the British Aluminium Co factory at Burntisland with a train of Presflo alumina and tank wagons for Thornton Yard just before the locomotive was condemned. Once so common around Fife, working from Thornton Junction and Dunfermline sheds, only three 'J38s' survived into 1967, and the last two went in April that year.

Upper left: With a clear view across the Firth of Forth to Edinburgh, Class B1 4-6-0 No 61330 heads north along the coast near Kinghorn with the 4.30pm Rosyth Dockyard–Thornton Junction workmen's train in September 1965.

Lower left: Resplendent in a new coat of paint — 'a condition she did not long remain in', as Bill observed when he sent this photograph in to *Trains Illustrated* — Gresley Class V2 2-6-2 No 60958 leaves Kirkcaldy at 5.29pm with a Dundee Tay Bridge–Edinburgh Waverley semi-fast in May 1957.

Right: Another photograph of the 4.30pm Rosyth Dockyard–Thornton Junction workmen's train, seen from the signalbox arriving at the nicely tended Dysart station behind BR Standard Class 4MT 2-6-0 No 76111 in August 1964. Only three of these engines were ever allocated to Thornton Junction, and by this date No 76111 was the sole example. Note Bill's Sunbeam Rapier motor car parked by the station gate.

76111
DYSART

60087

Left: In the summer of 1961 Class A3 Pacific No 60087 *Blenheim* passes Thornton Junction with the 1.42pm Aberdeen–King's Cross fish train while 'J39' 0-6-0 No 64792 passes underneath with a freight train from Methil to Thornton Yard. A number of passenger carriages, made redundant by the introduction of diesel multiple-units, can be seen stored either side of the station.

Upper right: Another view of No 64792, as it approaches Thornton Junction with a local train from Leven *c*1960. Today this scene has changed totally: the station has been rebuilt in a new location, and the 'bing' has disappeared.

Lower right: One of the LNER Class D11/2 4-4-0s of Robinson Great Central Railway design, No 62684 *Wizard of the Moor* of Eastfield shed waits to leave Thornton Junction with a stopping train for Glasgow Queen Street in 1957. Note the ash-and-sleeper construction of the platform — an effort to overcome the terrible problem of mining subsidence at this location.

Upper left: The first of the Reid North British 'Glen' Class D34 4-4-0s, No 62467 *Glenfinnan*, runs alongside the Firth of Forth as it approaches Largo with an empty-stock train, formed of LMS and LNER non-corridor stock, from Crail to Thornton Junction in August 1957. This location, known by them as the Yellow House beach, was a favourite spot for the Anderson family to go swimming.

Lower left: A year later and *Glenfinnan* is seen again as it arrives at Kilconquhar with a Thornton Junction–Crail train formed of rather more comfortable Gresley LNER teak corridor carriages and one BR Mk 1 carriage on 20 September 1958.

Right: Rebuilt Holmes NBR Class J36 0-6-0 No 65309 crosses the River Eden as it leaves Guard Bridge station on the five-mile journey from Leuchars Junction to St Andrews on a September afternoon in 1954.

64491

Left: Fitted with a snowplough, Class J35 0-6-0 No 64491 shunts a long train of empty coal wagons at Rothes Colliery in spring 1962. This modern colliery, which had opened in 1952, was to be closed in 1962after the sea flooded the workings.

Right: One of the shed men at Thornton Junction has the unenviable task of cleaning ash from the smokebox of former WD Austerity 2-8-0 No 90441 on a blustery day in March 1963. Thornton shed had a roster of a dozen of these powerful engines for the heaviest mineral duties around the Fife coalfield.

Left: Gresley Class J38 0-6-0 No 65908 blackens the already threatening sky as it passes the closed station at Falkland Road — between Ladybank and Markinch, on the climb to Lochmuir Summit — with a southbound mixed freight for Thornton Yard in the spring of 1961. Falkland Road station had closed in September 1958.

Right: Another of Thornton's WD 2-8-0s, No 90468 is working hard as it curves away from Thornton Yard with a train of coal empties for Westfield opencast site in the summer of 1964. This is one of the few large-format colour transparencies that Bill took using his Linhof camera.

90468

Left: The Edinburgh–Dundee main line crosses the backbone of Fife at Lochmuir Summit, where in steam days there was a loop to recess slower trains. Unusually, in this photograph taken *c*1964 WD 2-8-0 No 90117, with a northbound freight loaded mostly with coal, is overtaking BR Standard Caprotti Class 5MT 4-6-0 No 73145 from St Rollox shed, standing in the loop with another mixed goods.

Upper right: Still with 'L N E R' on its tender, Gresley Class D49 4-4-0 No 62725 *Inverness-shire* approaches Lochmuir Summit *c*1950 with a southbound farm-removal special conveying cattle and farm machinery.

Lower right: On 29 November 1952 the exhaust from Gresley Class K3 2-6-0 No 61885 hangs in the cold air as the locomotive passes Lochmuir signalbox with a northbound fitted freight. Both photographs on this page were taken with the Voigtlander camera, while that opposite was probably one of the last taken on the glass plate camera.

Upper left: Drummond Caledonian Railway 'Jumbo' Class 2F 0-6-0 No 57473 makes a nice picture as it accelerates away from Ladybank with the 6.2pm train for Perth in September 1955 — shortly before the sparse passenger service was withdrawn. There were only two trains each way per day, on weekdays only. This engine has a North British chimney from a Class J36 0-6-0, fitted during repairs at Inverurie Works. Nowadays, following closure of the Glenfarg route to Perth, this line once again sees passenger trains.

Lower left: Not quite in Fife, Reid NBR 'Scott' Class 'D30' 4-4-0 No 62436 *Lord Glenvarloch* sets off from Kinross Junction with the 4.25pm Perth to Glasgow Queen Street train which had come via Glenfarg and is taking the Devon Valley line via Rumbling Bridge to Alloa c1950.

Right: With West Lomond Hill just visible in the left background, Gresley Class A4 Pacific No 60011 *Empire of India* accelerates out of the curve through Ladybank with the morning Edinburgh Waverley–Aberdeen express *c*1951. The engine is in the short-lived light-blue livery applied to the 'A4s' in 1949/50.

60011

Left: Snow muffles the sound of WD 2-8-0 No 90199 from Eastfield shed as it reaches the top of the eight-mile climb from Inverkeithing at Crossgates and heads for Cowdenbeath with a train of coal empties bound probably for Thornton Yard during the freezing weather of early 1963.

Below: Also during the big freeze that gripped the nation in the first three months of 1963, snowplough-fitted Gresley Class J38 0-6-0 No 65932 shunts at Leslie prior to reversing its train down into Fettykil paper mill behind the shunter, who is changing the points. Notice Bill's car once again just behind the engine.

Left: In perfect silhouette, a Class J38 0-6-0 crosses the viaduct as it leaves Leslie bound for Markinch and Thornton Yard with coal empties and loaded vans from the Smith, Anderson & Co Fettykil paper mill at dusk one evening in February 1964.

Right: Another photograph taken at Leslie, with 'J38' No 65904 shunting the Fettykil paper-mill siding in April 1959. Note the stacks of pulp waiting to be processed and the Sunbeam Rapier ready for the off.

62677
62677
OCHILTREE

Left: Class D11/2 4-4-0 No 62677 *Edie Ochiltree,* from Dunfermline shed, was in its final month of service as it passed Lumphinnans East Junction with the 5.45pm Thornton Junction–Dunfermline train on 8 August 1959. It was probably the only member of its class to receive the later BR emblem on its tender.

Upper right: Another photograph taken at Lumphinnans East Junction of an up freight, this time headed by Class B1 4-6-0 No 61099 on an August evening in 1957. The train is signalled to take the old route to Cowdenbeath used latterly only by goods trains, a new line having been built for passenger trains to save the need for two stations in that town.

Lower right: One of the three Thornton BR Standard Class 4MT 2-6-0s, No 76109 heads the 1.50pm Thornton Junction–Dunfermline train between Cardenden and Lochgelly in April 1959.

Left: Class B1 4-6-0 No 61101 heads back up the Charlestown branch with a short goods train in February 1963. This branch from Elbowend Junction (between Dunfermline Lower and Cairneyhill) to the harbour at Charlestown was once very busy with coal for shipment and also for feeding the important lime kilns there. By this date, however, grass was encroaching on the track, and the line closed in February the following year.

Above: In an earlier view, Class J35 0-6-0 No 64525 is well prepared for bad weather, being fitted with a small plough, as it leaves Charlestown on the return journey to Elbowend Junction and civilisation with the daily goods train in February 1962. Yet again, the Sunbeam Rapier is waiting to chase the train to a spot further up the branch.

Above: Almost at the end of steam in Scotland, an unidentified WD 2-8-0 makes a dramatic start from Kinglassie Colliery *en route* to Thornton Junction with a loaded train of pulverised coal, destined probably for Kincardine power station, in March 1967. By this date just five of these engines were still at work from Thornton and Dunfermline sheds, both of which closed at the end of April.

Right: BR Standard Class 4MT 2-6-0 No 76109, still at work early in 1966, was captured on film as it came across the Lochore causeway with a loaded coal train on the Mary Pit branch heading towards Kelty. Not an entirely suitable type of locomotive for working heavy coal trains, it had been allocated to Dunfermline shed since January 1960 and was condemned in September 1966.

76109

61993

The Glenfarg Line

Left: The Glenfarg line, once the principal route from Edinburgh to Perth, was a particular favourite of Bill's, with its lovely scenery and steep gradient coming south. With the transfer of the Gresley Class K4 2-6-0s to Thornton Junction from Eastfield shed, some interesting photographic opportunities arose. Here No 61993 *Loch Long* storms up the 1-in-75 gradient from Bridge of Earn with a southbound train of coal empties from Perth on a frosty afternoon in October 1959.

Upper right: A stranger in the form of BR Standard 'Clan' Class 6MT 4-6-2, No 72006 *Clan Mackenzie* from Carlisle Kingmoor shed is seen near Milnathort with an evening Perth–Edinburgh Waverley train in August 1963. The Lomond Hills, known also as the 'Paps' of Fife, are prominent in the background.

Lower right: A train photographed by Bill probably more often than any other was the 4.5pm Edinburgh Waverley–Perth, which passed Glenfarg at approximately 5.30pm. Here Peppercorn Class A1 Pacific No 60161 *North British* races along near Blairadam in August 1961. Although this train had only six stops in its journey, it was always a Class B, despite usually being hauled by one of Haymarket's best Pacifics, but its timing was rather slow, at approximately 1hr 40min for the $47\frac{3}{4}$ miles.

Above: Class A1 4-6-2 No 60159 *Bonnie Dundee* has passed Glenfarg station and is reaching the summit of the climb from Bridge of Earn with the evening Perth–London Holloway car sleeper train in the summer of 1961. This train left Perth at 8pm on weekdays and 7.40pm on Sunday evenings. Sadly the Glenfarg line was closed between Cowdenbeath and Bridge of Earn in January 1970. Today this location lies beneath the tarmac of the M90 motorway, and the once peaceful countryside is shattered by the continual roar of traffic.

Right: Looking in the opposite direction at the same spot as the photograph above must have been Bill's favourite location on the gently rising gradient between Mawcarse Junction and Glenfarg. Although he took lots of black-and-white photographs here, this view of Gresley 'A3' 4-6-2 No 60099 *Call Boy* with the 4.5pm Edinburgh Waverley–Perth in the summer of 1962 is one of the very few colour transparencies. The 'Paps' of Fife dominate the background, with West Lomond Hill prominent on the left.

60099

Left: The big freeze of 1963 started over the New Year holiday, and on 3 January many diesel workings had to be covered by steam. Here Class A3 Pacific No 60100 *Spearmint* is nearing Glenfarg station with an express from Edinburgh Waverley to Perth. At that time most trains still had steam heating, and the boilers on the diesels gave a great deal of trouble in freezing weather.

Right: Possibly on the same day, Class B1 4-6-0 No 61292 from Dunfermline shed passes through Glenfarg station, where the platforms have been carefully cleared of snow, with a southbound train of coal empties from Perth.

Left: On a freezing day early in 1962, with icicles clinging to the rocks on the cutting side, Gresley Class V2 2-6-2 No 60883 storms Glenfarg Bank with the 12.5pm Perth–Edinburgh Waverley, which included through carriages from Inverness. What a wonderful sound this three-cylinder engine must have made as it climbed the 1-in-75 at a location where absolute quiet could be guaranteed.

Below: Under an azure sky, another 'V2', No 60894, runs easily between Mawcarse and Glenfarg with a Niddrie–Perth fitted freight early in 1962. This is another colour photograph taken in Bill's favourite location, but he had to move forward due to encroaching shadows and to try to keep below the exhaust which is being swept over the train by a biting northeast wind.

45165

Left: On a perfect summer afternoon, Stanier Class 5MT 4-6-0 No 45165 leaves the second of the two tunnels on the climb to Glenfarg station with a Perth–Glasgow Queen Street train formed of Gresley LNER teak carriages in the earlier BR 'blood and custard' livery *c*1956/7. It was the practice at some sheds — in this case Perth — to paint the backgrounds of smokebox numberplates either red or blue.

Right: The 4.5pm Edinburgh Waverley–Perth passes Milepost 26 near Kelty, between Cowdenbeath and Kinross Junction behind Peppercorn Class A1 Pacific No 60159 *Bonnie Dundee* in the spring of 1961. The Pacific is looking much cleaner than in the photograph on page 52.

Left: With heavy frost still on the sleepers, WD 2-8-0 No 90513 heads away from the camera as it climbs Glenfarg Bank with a southbound train of coal empties from Perth late in 1961.

Right: On a summer's evening in 1963 an unidentified WD 2-8-0 hammers up Glenfarg Bank as it climbs away from Strathearn with a southbound train of coal empties. Some of these wagons would most likely have been worked down from the Highlands and would be heading for the collieries of Fife.

46105
30

Hilton Junction

Left: Hilton Junction is the gateway to Perth from the south where the former Caledonian line from Glasgow and the south met the North British line from Edinburgh. Here LMS 'Rebuilt Royal Scot' 4-6-0 No 46105 *Cameron Highlander*, from Polmadie shed, takes the Glasgow route with the 12.15pm Perth–London Euston express (with through carriages from Aberdeen) in September 1960.

Right: BR Standard 'Britannia' 4-6-2 No 70020 *Mercury* leaves Moncrieff Tunnel at the approach to Hilton Junction with the 4.45pm fish train from Perth to the South in June 1962. This train originated from Aberdeen at 2.10pm, stopped for examination in Perth station (where some vans were either added or removed) and a fresh locomotive took over which worked through to Carlisle.

Upper left: Another interesting train which came from Aberdeen and went south via the Caledonian route was the 'Up Special TPO' (Travelling Post Office), often referred to as the West Coast Postal and seen passing Hilton Junction behind recently ex-works Class A3 Pacific No 60037 *Hyperion* on a June evening in 1962. This engine had recently returned to St Margaret's shed after a general repair at Doncaster Works but was an unusual choice of locomotive for this train. Later in July, when two 'A3s' were also allocated to St Rollox, they could be seen regularly on this turn.

Lower left: With its chime whistle sounding a warning, Gresley Class A4 4-6-2 No 60031 *Golden Plover* approaches Hilton Junction with the 5pm Glasgow Buchanan Street–Dundee West express, formed of LMS stock. This was the first of two 'A4s' to be transferred to St Rollox — this one in February and No 60027 *Merlin* in May 1962 — which worked Dundee trains and occasionally the Aberdeen three-hour expresses, which were then being put in the hands of 'A4s' transferred to Ferryhill shed, Aberdeen.

Right: Class B1 4-6-0 No 61330 approaches Hilton Junction on the former North British line from Bridge of Earn in the spring of 1963 with a short freight train which may have come off the Newburgh line at Bridge of Earn.

Perth

Below: An evening scene at Perth General, with Stanier 'Black Five' No 44997 — a Perth engine equipped with a tablet-exchanger for working north to Inverness — waiting to leave with an unidentified northbound express in June 1961. Caledonian Class 2F 0-6-0T No 56347 pauses between station-pilot duties.

Right: An atmospheric photograph showing an unidentified LMS 'Rebuilt Royal Scot' 4-6-0 leaving Perth General with the 9pm sleeping-car express to London Euston on a late-summer evening in 1963. This train included a through sleeping car from Oban on Saturday nights in summer and Monday nights in winter.

M14008

Left: Superpower for the 10.20am Aberdeen–Euston express, seen passing Friarton level crossing as it leaves Perth behind Stanier 'Black Five' No 44954 and 'Coronation' Pacific No 46226 *Duchess of Norfolk* in the autumn of 1961. This train departed from Perth at 12.20pm after changing engines and was due into London at 10.16pm. (Note: The timings given for these long-distance trains often changed slightly from summer to winter etc and according to the day of the week. As Bill did not often record the exact date of his photographs, readers must bear with us if the details are not exactly correct.)

Right: BR Standard Caprotti Class 5MT 4-6-0 No 73147 makes a dramatic departure from Perth with a Dundee West–Glasgow Buchanan Street express in the winter of 1961/2. These engines were the mainstay of this service for several years, 10 of them being allocated for this purpose to St Rollox shed from new in 1957 until 1965/6.

Left: Gresley Class V2 2-6-2 No 60804 leaves Perth with a Dundee West–Glasgow Buchanan Street express during the winter of 1961/2. This was when Perth was being re-signalled; the train is passing the old semaphore signals, while those on the down line are already out of use, replaced by the colour-light signals alongside. This engine was the first of this class to be allocated to a Scottish shed when sent brand-new to Dundee in November 1936.

Upper right: The southbound 'Up Special TPO' leaves Perth behind Thompson Class A2/3 4-6-2 No 60524 *Herringbone* for the journey to Carstairs, where it joined with Glasgow and Edinburgh portions for Euston, in September 1963. This was one of six 'A2s' most surprisingly transferred officially to Polmadie shed in October 1963.

Lower right: Stanier 'Black Five' 4-6-0 No 45363 approaches Perth General with a parcels train from Carlisle in the spring of 1962. Steam from a locomotive blowing off at Perth shed can be seen on the far right, while on the left the re-signalling is still not complete on the up side; note the colour-light signal covered with sacking.

Above: Bill sometimes visited Perth shed in the late afternoon to see what might be working the fish and other southbound trains and uncharacteristically took a few photographs of engines on shed while talking to drivers to arrange some smoke *en route*! Stanier 'Princess Royal' Pacific No 46203 *Princess Margaret Rose* is turned ready to work the 9pm sleeper in June 1962.

Upper left: Grimy 'A3' Pacific No 60089 *Felstead* stands beside 'Black Five' No 44784, fitted with a large snowplough, in the spring of 1962. This latter engine was in the process of being transferred from Inverness, where steam had just finished, to Ayr.

Lower left: In July 1963 Class 6MT 'Clan' Pacific No 72007 *Clan Mackintosh* receives attention from its driver before working the 4.45pm fish train as 'A1' Pacific No 60162 *Saint Johnstoun* waits in the foreground to take an evening train to Edinburgh.

Upper right: Crimson Class 8P 'Coronation' Pacific No 46247 *City of Liverpool* has been well coaled up and is getting ready to reverse off shed at Perth to work the 9pm sleeper to Euston as far as Carlisle in the summer of 1961.

Lower right: Gresley 'K4' 2-6-0 No 61995 *Cameron of Lochiel*, standing by the Edinburgh Road bridge, has probably come from the coaling tower and is preparing to back down to the turntable before taking a train of coal empties south on the Glenfarg line in 1960.

Below: Fowler LMS Class 4F 0-6-0 No 44181, from Kingmoor shed and probably fresh from repair at Inverurie Works, stands on shed at Perth in 1961 with the coaling tower in the background.

PLATFORM
4 NORTH
END
45527

Left: In Perth station, LMS 'Rebuilt Patriot' 4-6-0 No 45527 *Southport* has just coupled onto the 4.45pm fish train for the South and is preparing for departure in July 1964. By this date the incidence of LMS Class 7 and 8 power on this train was decreasing as locomotives were withdrawn, and, indeed, the fish traffic itself would soon be lost to road transport. Once more, the Sunbeam Rapier waits to take Bill to Gleneagles, where *Southport* would be photographed again as it headed south (see page 110).

Right: Prompted by the abysmal performance of the 'D61xx' diesels built by North British, the Scottish Region had the bright idea of drafting in redundant Gresley 'A4' Pacifics to work the principal Aberdeen–Glasgow expresses. These included former King's Cross and Gateshead engines as well as those from Haymarket. Here, in a photograph taken with the Linhof camera, No 60010 *Dominion of Canada* departs Perth with the 5.30pm Buchanan Street–Aberdeen in the summer of 1964.

40938

Left: For many years Perth had a small stud of Fowler LMS Class 4P three-cylinder 4-4-0 compounds. Here nicely turned-out No 40938 is reduced to working a train of coal empties out of Perth in the Forfar direction on 29 August 1953. Quite why they were being taken this way when all the collieries lay in the other direction is unknown. All the compounds had left Perth by 1957.

Below: The summer of 1962 saw the last workings by Stanier 'Princess Royal' Pacifics. Here the first of the class, No 46200 *Princess Royal*, storms out of Perth at Friarton with the 4.45pm fish train for the South in September of that year. By November the last of the class, including *Princess Royal*, had been withdrawn, and the fish train was more often in the hands of a Class 6 or 7 locomotive.

Upper left: Stanier 'Black Five' 4-6-0 No 45499 crosses the River Tay by the single line bridge as it approaches Perth with the 12.0 Dundee West–Glasgow Buchanan Street in the spring of 1963.

Lower left: Crossing the River Tay in the opposite direction is Thompson Class B1 4-6-0 No 61277 as it leaves Perth with a freight train for Dundee on a spring afternoon in 1963.

Right: In a photograph printed from a large-format Linhof transparency, a BR Standard Caprotti Class 5MT 4-6-0 leaves Perth and crosses the River Tay with a late-afternoon Glasgow Buchanan Street–Dundee West train *c*1965/6. In the background can be seen the Grampian Mountains, and for this reason Perth is known as the Gateway to the Highlands.

60813

The Tay Bridge

Left: No 60813, the Gresley Class V2 2-6-2 that was unique in having a 'shovel-rim' deflector around its chimney, comes round the curve at Wormit as it leaves the Tay Bridge with the 12.10pm Dundee Tay Bridge–Edinburgh Millerhill express freight in April 1965.

Upper right: The 12.20pm Dundee Tay Bridge–Newport-on-Tay East local arrives at Wormit station behind tender-first Class B1 4-6-0 No 61102 in September 1964. Normally this service would have run through to Tayport, but at this time work was in progress on building the approach to the new Tay Road Bridge which disrupted services.

Lower right: In March 1966 Class A2 Pacific No 60530 *Sayajirao* — named after the Maharaja of Baroda's horse, which won the 1947 St Leger — crosses the last span of the Tay Bridge as it comes south with a brake van. This was one of three 'A2s' allocated to Dundee Tay Bridge in the last years of steam, mainly for fitted-freight work to Millerhill Yard.

RCTS SLS
SCOTTISH RAIL TOUR
G.N.S.R.
№ 49

Great North of Scotland Lines

Left: Preserved Great North of Scotland Railway Class D40 4-4-0 No 49 *Gordon Highlander* pilots the Highland Railway 'Jones Goods' 4-6-0 No 103 on the climb through Glen Fiddich from Craigellachie to Dufftown with the RCTS/SLS 'Scottish Rail Tour' on 16 June 1962. In earlier days Bill photographed several trains in this location during his National Service at RAF Kinloss.

Below: Class 'J36' 0-6-0 No 65277 arrives at Carron station with the daily pick-up goods from Boat of Garten to Craigellachie on the 'Speyside line' in 1960. Andrew Barclay 0-4-0ST *Dailuaine* waits in the foreground to collect wagons for a local whisky distillery. In addition to the Andrew Barclay works plate on its cab side, *Dailuaine* also carries a plate stating that it is registered to run on British Railways tracks.

Left: One of the later Heywood GNSR Class D40 4-4-0s, No 62275 *Sir David Stuart,* makes a pleasing sight as it approaches Nethybridge with the 1pm train from Boat of Garten to Craigellachie in July 1955.

Right: Pickersgill GNSR Class D40 No 62267 departs from Ballindalloch with the 2.55pm Craigellachie–Boat of Garten in August 1955. There were only three trains each way on this line on weekdays, plus one extra late-evening train on Saturdays. The service could be managed by one engine, but as it started the day from Boat of Garten it was probably necessary to change engines during the course of a day.

62267
62267

Upper left: With the gradual scrapping of the GNSR 4-4-0s, replacements had to be found to work the Speyside line. These came in the form of two nearly new BR Standard Class '2MT' 2-6-0s — Nos 78053/4. The latter is seen here one mile west of Nethybridge with the 2.55pm Craigellachie–Boat of Garten in September 1957.

Lower left: Another type of 2-6-0 that could be seen on the Speyside line — usually on goods workings — were the Gresley Great Northern Class K2 Moguls. Here No 61792 shunts the 8.30am pick-up goods from Boat of Garten on the Balmenach Burn bridge at Cromdale in September 1957.

Right: The last surviving GNSR 4-4-0, Heywood Class D40 No 62277 *Gordon Highlander*, crosses Cullen Viaduct beside the North Sea with a Buchan-line pick-up goods for Keith on 28 September 1957. This was one of its very last workings before entering Inverurie Works for restoration as GNSR No 49 and subsequent preservation.

62277

On Highland Lines

Below: In October 1956 the last former Highland Railway locomotive left in service with British Railways, Peter Drummond 0-4-4T No 55053, heads the 2.5pm mixed train from The Mound to Dornoch beside Loch Fleet near Skelbo, with Ben Lundie in the background. This engine received an overhaul at St Rollox Works in June 1956 and was repainted in the BR lined black livery. Sadly it broke its crank axle soon after this photograph was taken and was officially withdrawn in January 1957. There were only two return trips a day from Dornoch, where the engine was stabled, which made for very poor connections at The Mound with trains on the Far North line to Wick. The branch was closed in June 1960.

Right: The preserved Highland Railway 'Jones Goods' 4-6-0, No 103, about to depart from Kyle of Lochalsh with the 5.40pm train to Inverness during filming for the BBC Television *Railway Roundabout* programme in June 1961. The cattle wagons were probably added to the train to make it look a little more authentic. Beyond the buffer-stops a coastal vessel is sailing down Loch Alsh, while rising out of the water on the other side of the loch are the mountains of the Isle of Skye, the most prominent peak being Ben na Caillich. Clearly a cautious approach to this terminus is recommended! No 103 was the first 4-6-0 built for service in the UK, being the first of 15 built by Sharp, Stewart & Co in 1894.

H.R 103

45473

Left: The last regular passenger steam workings on the Highland lines north of Inverness were the mail trains to Kyle of Lochalsh. Here Stanier 'Black Five' 4-6-0 No 45473 climbs the 1-in-50 gradient just west of Lochluichart at the start of the 14-mile ascent to Luib Summit with the 10.40am from Inverness in May 1961.

Right: McIntosh Caledonian Railway Class 3F 0-6-0 No 57587 climbs the 1-in-70 from Lairg as it makes its way home to Helmsdale with a northbound permanent-way train on Friday 9 September 1955.

Upper left: Cumming Highland Railway 'Clan Goods' 4-6-0 No 57956, still with 'L M S' on its tender, crosses the River Ness Viaduct as it leaves Inverness with a freight train for Kyle of Lochalsh in March 1951. Bill later commented that this photograph was taken from the steps of a rather seedy tenement, which, on reflection, was probably the local 'red light' district, in view of its proximity to the harbour!

Lower left: Prior to June 1960 there was a local service from Inverness to Tain. These trains were usually worked by Pickersgill CR Class 3P 4-4-0s such as No 54470, seen leaving Inverness past Clachnaharry signalbox after crossing the swing bridge over the Caledonian Canal with the 3pm train to Tain in May 1952. The Moray Firth is in the background and the Black Isle beyond.

Right: A very typical scene on the Highland main line. With safety valves lifting, a pair of Stanier 'Black Fives' — Nos 44975 and 45462 — begin the long climb from Inverness to the 1,013ft Slochd Summit with the heavy 3.40pm to Perth (with through carriages to Glasgow Buchanan Street and Edinburgh Waverley) under a stormy sky on Saturday 22 March 1952. Note the second vehicle, which is a former Highland Railway TPO.

44975

Below: There were two routes south from Inverness to Aviemore — the old line via Forres and the new line over Slochd. Here, on the old line, 'Black Five' No 44925 has just crossed Dunphail Viaduct on the 17-mile climb from Forres to Dava Moor (1,052ft) in September 1957 with the 5.20pm from Forres. At Aviemore this train joined with the 'Royal Highlander', which travelled by the new line, leaving Inverness at 5.40pm. Note the 12-wheeled LNWR-style sleeping car, which went through to Euston. This line was closed in October 1965.

Right: BR Standard Class 5MT 4-6-0 No 73106, one of a pair allocated to Inverness from June to October 1957, comes round the great curve after crossing Slochd Viaduct, seen above the first carriage of the train, on the climb to Slochd Summit with the 3.5pm Aviemore–Inverness in September 1957. Northbound trains faced a climb of 11 miles after a dip just before Carr Bridge, but this was easier than the southbound climb of an almost unbroken 20 miles.

73106

54484
54484

Left: Many trains took on pilots at Aviemore for the climb over Slochd Summit, and in this photograph Pickersgill Class 3P 4-4-0 No 54484 pilots 'Black Five' No 45461 early in the morning between Aviemore and Carr Bridge with the summer 9.55pm York–Inverness 'Highlands Car Sleeper' train in August 1959. Arrival at Inverness was scheduled for 7.35am.

Above: At Aviemore a station pilot was employed to detach and attach the Forres portions from Perth–Inverness trains and *vice versa*. Here McIntosh CR Class 2P 0-4-4T No 55173 is shunting the Forres portion of the southbound 'Royal Highlander' onto the main train for the overnight journey to Euston while at the other end the train engine is blowing off ready for the climb to Druimuachdar.

Left: 'Black Five' 4-6-0 No 45171 slogs up the 1-in-70 gradient near Dalnacardoch on the climb to the 1,484ft summit at Druimuachdar with the 8am Perth–Inverness freight in July 1957. Banking assistance from Blair Atholl is being provided by a Fairburn LMS 2-6-4T. There were three of these tanks at Perth which were sub-shedded at Blair Atholl for this work; they were later replaced by BR Standard 2-6-4Ts.

Right: The 3.40pm Inverness–Perth approaches Druimuachdar Summit from the north behind a pair of 'Black Fives', with No 45367 leading, *c*1955. The Highland TPO is the first vehicle in the train. Note the 'feather' at the safety valves of both engines — so typical of how well these hard-working Highland engines steamed.

45367

45460

Left: The hard work is almost over as a pair of 'Black Five' 4-6-0s — Nos 45460 and 45366 — climb the last serious gradient from Dunkeld to Kingswood Tunnel, near the site of Rohallion Halt, with the 11am Inverness–Perth *c*1955.

Upper right: The handful of local trains between Perth and Blair Atholl were worked mostly by Caledonian Pickersgill 4-4-0s. However, the Fairburn 2-6-4Ts based at Blair Atholl also took a turn when spare from banking work. Here Class 4MT 2-6-4T No 42169 leaves Ballinluig with the 9.25am Perth–Blair Atholl in October 1958.

Lower right: In 1954 a pair of brand-new Swindon-built BR Standard Class 3MT 2-6-0s were allocated to Perth for the local traffic on the Highland line. Here No 77008 heads the 1.35pm Perth–Blair Atholl local through the woods near Dunkeld on Saturday 15 May 1954. These two engines did not stay long, being reallocated to Polmadie in December the same year.

Upper left: For many years the Aberfeldy branch was worked by McIntosh CR Class 2P 0-4-4Ts. Here No 55217 speeds down the Tay Valley near Grandtully with the 12.0 mixed train from Aberfeldy to Ballinluig on a snowy day in January 1960.

Lower left: By 1962 there were few McIntosh 0-4-4Ts left at work, and in May that year No 80092 — one of the BR Standard Class 4MT 2-6-4Ts previously used for banking duties at Blair Atholl — is seen departing from Ballinluig with the 1.8pm train to Aberfeldy; this branch closed in 1965. Once again the Sunbeam Rapier waits in the station yard, this time with skis on the roof, though it would seem unlikely that there was any snow left above Aviemore!

Right: Pickersgill Class 3P 4-4-0 No 54494 leaves the tunnel and enters the passing loop at Kingswood with a Blair Atholl–Perth pick-up goods in October 1958. This was another favourite train for Bill to photograph — until brand-new BR/Sulzer Type 2 diesel No D5125 turned up in October 1960. He did, however, take a good photo of the diesel, which appeared in *Trains Illustrated.*

54494

Perth to Stirling

Below: BR Standard Caprotti Class 5MT 4-6-0 No 73151 races down from Gleneagles to Hilton Junction over the River Earn near Forgandenny with a northbound extra *c*1960. The greatest distraction for photographers along this stretch of line was the heavy-duty telephone cable, visible on the left.

Right: In August 1964 BR Standard 'Britannia' 4-6-2 No 70011 *Hotspur* approaches Hilton Junction with the 1.26pm Carlisle–Perth. This train always brought one of the larger passenger engines from Kingmoor to Perth. The North British line from Bridge of Earn can be seen curving in on the left.

Left: An unidentified Class A4 Pacific glints in the low autumn sunlight as it sprints past Blackford with an express from Glasgow Buchanan Street to Aberdeen or Dundee in October 1963.

Right: Another unidentified locomotive — a BR Standard Class 5MT 4-6-0 — glints as it comes down from Gleneagles with a northbound express in September 1963. Unfortunately Bill did not record which locomotives were on either of these trains or exactly where the Standard 4-6-0 was taken. Here Bill was obviously experimenting with the lighting, hoping for the much sought-after 'glint' shot.

Below: At Gleneagles station in June 1963 a permanent-way gang pause in their work as Drummond Caledonian 'Jumbo' 0-6-0 No 57261 shunts the daily Perth–Stirling pick-up goods into the yard past the very fine signal gantry that controlled access to the Crieff line.

Right: A very nicely turned-out Stanier 'Black Five' 4-6-0, No 44725 from Kingmoor, makes black smoke as it departs from Gleneagles with the 3.30pm Aberdeen–Glasgow Buchanan Street express, possibly on the same day in June 1963.

44725

Above: 'Rebuilt Patriot' Class 6P 4-6-0 No 45527 *Southport* has just passed Gleneagles with the 4.45pm fish train from Perth in July 1964. This is the same train as illustrated on page 74, which Bill has chased in his Sunbeam Rapier car. Glen Eagles itself can be seen in the left background, with the 1,592ft Steele's Knowe above.

Right: With the Ochil Hills in the background, the 1.26pm Carlisle–Perth train slows for its stop at Gleneagles, hauled by 'Clan' Pacific No 72005 *Macgregor* from Kingmoor shed *c*1964. The five Scottish examples of this class, allocated to Polmadie shed, were all withdrawn in December 1962, but the five Kingmoor examples remained at work until 1965/6, mostly on trains into Scotland.

72005

44923

Left: With the Ochil Hills again in the background, Stanier 'Black Five' No 44923 rounds the curve about a mile and a half south of Gleneagles on a wonderfully fresh and clear winter morning with a southbound Christmas parcels train in December 1963.

Below: Class A2 4-6-2 No 60532 *Blue Peter* storms southbound through Blackford with the Sunday-morning Dundee West–Glasgow Buchanan Street express on another clear frosty January day in 1964. This engine was normally kept on standby at Dundee but was exercised once a week on this train.

Upper left: 'Britannia' Pacific No 70001 *Lord Hurcomb* passes the closed station at Kinbuck, the summit of the six-mile bank that starts one mile south of Bridge of Allan, with the 1.26pm Carlisle–Perth train in March 1965. This station had closed in June 1956.

Lower left: Well-cleaned Standard Class 4MT 2-6-4T No 80122 leaves Stirling with the 3.39pm fast for Edinburgh Princes Street in September 1961. This engine was allocated to Dalry Road (64C) at this time but carries a 66C (Hamilton) shedplate.

Right: 'Rebuilt Patriot' 4-6-0 No 45530, formerly named *Sir Frank Ree,* climbs Kinbuck Bank 'by the bonnie banks o'Allan Water' past a Scout troop walking alongside the railway, soon after leaving Dunblane with the 1.26pm Carlisle–Perth in April 1965. One of the last LMS Class 7P locomotives to remain in service, it has been branded with a yellow stripe on its cab to denote that it was banned from working under the 25kV catenary south of Crewe. The safety authorities would throw a fit if a Scout troop took a short-cut along the lineside today!

46247
SHUNT LIMIT

Left: The 1.26pm Carlisle–Perth seen again in happier times. Crimson 'Coronation' Pacific No 46247 *City of Liverpool* approaches Dunblane in the summer of 1962.

Upper right: Standard Caprotti Class 5MT 4-6-0 No 73152 heads south from Stirling near Bannockburn with a Dundee West–Glasgow Buchanan Street train in late summer 1964. Stirling Castle can be seen in the background centre left.

Lower right: The scene at Stirling station at 7.4pm one evening in June 1963. Standard Class 5MT 4-6-0 No 73106 leaves with the 6.15pm Glasgow Buchanan Street–Callander as a DMU for Edinburgh Waverley (via Alloa and Dunfermline) waits to leave the bay platform.

The Callander & Oban Line

Below: CR McIntosh Class 2P 0-4-4T No 55204 stands in Killin station with the 11.5am branch train to Killin Junction on an arctic day in the winter of 1961/2. Note the engine crew in their Wellington boots!

Right: On the same day the sun is already sinking fast as BR Caprotti Class 5MT 4-6-0 No 73147 climbs near Luib, between Crianlarich and Killin Junction, with the 12.5pm Oban–Glasgow Buchanan Street.

73147

80028

Left: The Killin branch was also taken over by BR Standard Class 4MT 2-6-4Ts in the last years of its existence. Here No 80028, fitted with a tablet-exchanger, approaches Strathyre with the 4.5pm Callander–Killin school train in July 1965. Loch Lubnaig is in the background. Note the water spraying on the coal bunker to reduce the dust when the engine runs bunker-first to Killin from Killin Junction and also spilling off the end of the single Gresley LNER non-corridor brake.

Right: The 4.5pm Callander–Killin school train is seen again on an earlier occasion climbing through Glen Ogle with McIntosh Class 2P 0-4-4T No 55204 in charge during the summer of 1961. This was a most spectacular stretch of railway but a headache to the railway authorities, which had to keep a close watch for fallen rocks. It was a rockslide near this spot that led to the premature closure of the line, on 27 September 1965. On a happier note, it is now possible to traverse the trackbed through Glen Ogle, as this has now been opened up as a cycle- and footpath.

Above and right: Stanier 'Black Five' No 45049 is unusually piloting Thompson Class B1 4-6-0 No 61278 from Dundee shed on an Oban–Glasgow Buchanan Street train, seen approaching the summit at Glenoglehead in late spring 1961. Although 'Black Fives' were commonplace on the former NBR/LNER West Highland line, the appearance of a former LNER engine on the former CR/LMS Callander & Oban line was extremely rare.

45049

KILLIN JUNCTION
CHANGE FOR
KILLIN AND LOCH TAY
45124

Left: With safety valves roaring, Inverness 'Black Five' 4-6-0 No 45124 waits impatiently at Killin Junction for the single line to clear for its freight train for Oban on Monday 7 April 1952. In the left background the Killin-branch engine, No 55222, can just be seen running round its single-carriage train.

Upper right: BR Standard Class 4MT 2-6-4T No 80028 runs bunker-first down the Killin branch soon after leaving Killin Junction with the 2.46pm branch train from Killin Junction in June 1965.

Lower right: Another, longer branch off the Callander & Oban line was that from Connel Ferry to Ballachulish. Here a McIntosh 0-4-4T heads an evening train along the shore of Loch Linnhe near Kentallen with a train from Ballachulish *c*1952.

VICTORIA' HOTEL
H.A. SAUNDERS
HOTEL
HOTEL
44724

Left: Another line that joined the Callander & Oban at Balquhidder was that from Crieff, which was closed beyond Comrie in 1951. Here, in the spring of 1964, Stanier 'Black Five' No 44724 is preparing to back its two-carriage train out of the down platform and will re-enter the station by the up line in readiness for its return to Gleneagles. Several attempts were made to introduce railbuses on this line, but the steep grades seemed to be too much for them, and steam reigned supreme until the closure of this remnant of the line.

Below: At the Ballachulish terminus of the 27¾-mile branch from Connel Ferry, McIntosh 0-4-4T No 55260 removes a camping coach, freshly overhauled for the approaching summer season, that it has brought down with the branch train in the spring of 1962. This was one of 10 such engines of Caledonian design that were built for the LMS in 1925 by Nasmyth, Wilson & Co of Patricroft, Manchester. The 2,430ft Pap of Glencoe is very prominent, as are the remnants of the slate-mine working cut into the hillside.

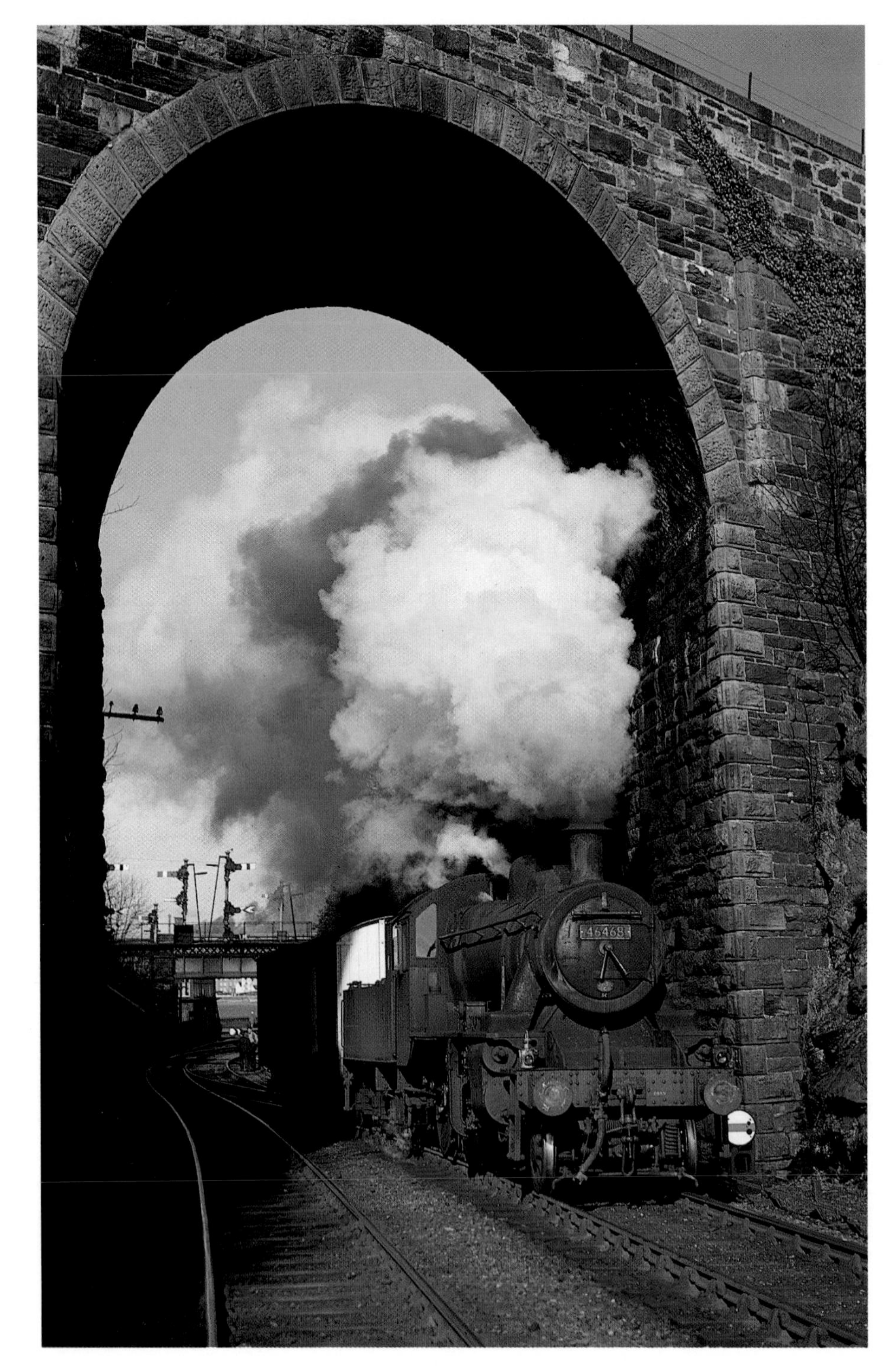

Left: Ivatt LMS Class 2MT 2-6-0 No 46468 shunts some fish vans outside Oban station in the spring of 1952. Oban was once a very busy terminus with a grand station and is still an important connecting point for the ferries to the islands off the West Coast. The blue water in the harbour can just be glimpsed through the bridge.

Above: On a cold morning in late 1961, McIntosh 0-4-4T No 55173 produces a dramatic cloud of smoke and steam as it climbs out of the mist that has lain all day with the 1.42pm Killin–Killin Junction train. This engine went for scrap in January 1962, having been allocated to Oban shed only since the previous September.

Right: Earlier the same day, Stanier 'Black Five' No 44879 climbs from Killin Junction towards Glenoglehead with the 9.30am Oban–Glasgow Buchanan Street train. Oban shed closed officially in July 1962, but occasional steam workings still made their way west until closure of the line between Dunblane and Crianlarich, whereupon trains to Oban were re-routed via the West Highland line.

44879

E16179
39
70

The West Highland Line

Left: A pair of former Great Northern Railway Gresley Class K2 2-6-0s, Nos 61783 *Loch Sheil* and 61789 *Loch Laidon*, leave Mallaig with an afternoon train for Fort William and Glasgow Queen Street in June 1950. Both engines are in postwar LNER apple-green livery, the leading one now lettered 'BRITISH RAILWAYS'.

Upper right: Probably on the same day, Gresley Class K4 2-6-0 No 61998 *Macleod of Macleod,* also in apple green, approaches Mallaig with a train from Fort William.

Lower right: Postwar Peppercorn Class K1 2-6-0 No 62031 and Gresley Class K2 2-6-0 No 61774 *Loch Garry* head a Mallaig–Fort William–Glasgow train near Lochailort *c*1955.

Left: In scenery typical of the Mallaig extension, the prototype Thompson LNER Class K1/1 2-6-0, No 61997 *MacCailin Mór*, heads the 12.30pm Mallaig–Fort William above the shores of Loch Eilt, between Lochailort and Glenfinnan, in the summer of 1955. This engine was a two-cylinder rebuild of a Gresley three-cylinder K4.

Right: Class K2 2-6-0 No 61791 *Loch Laggan* working hard on a freight train for Mallaig near Lochailort on Thursday 1 June 1950. These former Great Northern engines were first transferred to Scotland in 1924, and by 1932 20 had been sent north. In 1933/4 the 13 that regularly worked over the West Highland line were named after lochs situated near to the line; one, BR No 61783 (illustrated on page 130), named after Loch Shiel, had its name incorrectly spelt *Loch Sheil*.

44957

Left: Stanier 'Black Five' 4-6-0 No 44957 and another member of the class burst from a short tunnel at Fersit between Tulloch and Rannoch with a Fort William to Glasgow Queen Street train c1958. Both engines would be from Eastfield shed where ten of these LMS design engines were kept specifically for working on the West Highland line.

Below: Shadows lengthen as another 'Black Five', No 44968 and Gresley Class K2 2-6-0 No 61774 *Loch Garry*, head the 4.35pm Glasgow Queen Street to Fort William train on the last part of the eight mile climb from Ardlui as they near Crianlarich into the approaching night c1958. In the old North British Railway tradition, the assisting engine is coupled behind the train engine.

73077

Left: One of the five BR Standard Class 5MT 4-6-0s allocated to Eastfield shed for service on the West Highland line, No 73077 pilots a Stanier 'Black Five' on the 1pm Mallaig–Glasgow Queen Street train as they drop down from the highest summit on the line, between Bridge of Orchy and Tyndrum Upper, in March 1956.

Right: The Arrochar–Craigendoran push-pull train is seen high above Loch Long in the charge of Reid NBR Class C15 4-4-2T No 67460 in May 1958. This was one of a pair of these tank engines retained for working this service until replaced by a railbus in April 1960 and nicknamed 'Yorkies', having been built by the Yorkshire Engine Co in the years 1911-13.

Left: Steam had all but finished on the West Highland line by December 1962, when Fort William shed was closed. However, the SLS organised a special train from Glasgow to Mallaig on 1 June 1963 to mark the end. Here the preserved Reid NBR 'Glen' class 4-4-0 No 256 *Glen Douglas* and 'J37' 0-6-0 No 64632 head the 'Jacobite' railtour through Glen Falloch on the outward journey to Fort William. The 'J37' ran hot and had to be removed from the train at Rannoch, and a diesel was requisitioned from a freight train to assist the 'Glen' to Fort William.

Right: From Fort William to Mallaig the 'Jacobite' was hauled by a pair of Class J37 0-6-0s, Nos 64592 and 64636, seen here storming away from Glenfinnan. Both had hot bearings on arrival at Mallaig, and the entire return journey was made behind a diesel.

64592

Glasgow

Upper left: Bill rarely visited Glasgow — or South West Scotland, for that matter — but he did spend a few minutes on Eglinton Street station on the former Caledonian line out of Glasgow Central in 1956. Here BR Standard Class 4MT 2-6-4T No 80002 approaches the station with a Glasgow Central–Motherwell local as Fowler LMS Class 2P 4-4-0 No 40609 crosses over the top in the background as it approaches Cumberland Street station with a local for St Enoch.

Lower left: Looking the other way at Eglinton Street on the same day in 1956, well-polished McIntosh Class 2P 0-4-4T No 55265 — one of those built for the LMS in 1925 by Nasmyth, Wilson — has been checked in the station with an empty-stock train for Glasgow Central.

Right: A view of the former Glasgow & South Western Railway terminus at Glasgow St Enoch. In the spring of 1964 Standard Class 4MT 2-6-4T No 80020 leaves with a local train as another member of the class, No 80106, waits to reverse out of the station after being released from its train.

44672

Left: An interesting view of the architecture at St Enoch, with Stanier 'Black Five' No 44672 waiting to leave with the 5.30pm stopping train to Carlisle in April 1965.

Upper right: Dereliction is already setting in at Buchanan Street station as BR Standard Caprotti Class 5MT 4-6-0 No 73153 departs with the 6.15pm for Dundee West in September 1964.

Lower right: At St Enoch No 80106, already seen on page 141, has now reversed out and is running back ready to couple onto another evening rush-hour train in the spring of 1964.

The West Coast Main Line

Below: 'Rebuilt Royal Scot' 4-6-0 No 46118 *Royal Welch Fusilier*, from Crewe North shed, passes under the fine signal gantry at Carstairs as it enters the station with a southbound Anglo-Scottish express from Glasgow Central *c*1958.

Right: One of the final BR Standard 'Britannia' Pacifics to be built, No 70051 *Firth of Forth* hurries south two miles north of Abington, with the Tinto Hills in the background, at the head of a Glasgow–Manchester express in August 1958.

70051

Left: In a momentary patch of sunlight, an unidentified 'Rebuilt Royal Scot' 4-6-0 is seen south of Beattock station with a southbound express (1M52) on a summer evening in 1961.

Below: On a rather more stormy looking day in the summer of 1962, Stanier 'Coronation' Pacific No 46237 *City of Bristol* heads a northbound Anglo-Scottish express (1S51) soon after passing Beattock Summit.

Upper left: BR Standard Class 3MT 2-6-0 No 77005 brings a northbound parcels round the curve from Beattock Summit during the summer of 1961.

Lower left: 'Britannia' Pacific No 70044 *Earl Haig* blackens the sky as it passes through Crawford station, with its typical Caledonian Railway signalbox, at the head of a southbound express (1M32) in the summer of 1963.

Right: A much less grand signalbox is seen at Law Junction as Stanier LMS 'Jubilee' 4-6-0 No 45717 *Dauntless*, from Bank Hall shed, passes with the 1.45pm Glasgow Central–Liverpool Exchange express in May 1961.

45717
50

42780

Left: LMS Hughes/Fowler 'Crab' 2-6-0 No 42780 of Grangemouth shed passes Beattock Summit with a northbound express freight *c*1957. Note the steam from the banking engine giving the train a final shove before dropping back and crossing over to return light engine back down the bank to Beattock shed. Note also the snow fencing fashioned out of old sleepers — very necessary in this exposed location.

Below: An extremely rare pairing of both types of former WD locomotive: 2-10-0 No 90774 and an unidentified 2-8-0 pass Beattock Summit with a southbound freight in June 1957. No 90774 was the last of the 150 2-10-0s built for the War Department in 1943-5 and at one time carried the name *North British*. Only 25 were taken into BR stock, as opposed to 733 2-8-0s.

Left: BR 'Clan' Pacific No 72009 *Clan Stewart* rounds the curve through Crawford with just over five miles to go on the rather gentler climb to Beattock Summit from the north with an express from Glasgow in the summer of 1961.

Right: In the summer of 1963 'Coronation' Pacific No 46244 *King George VI* climbs the 1-in-74/76 past Greskine signal-box, roughly halfway up Beattock Bank, with a Euston–Glasgow Central express.

46244

Above: At Harthope Stanier 'Black Five' 4-6-0 No 45076, from Newton Heath shed, Manchester, keeps a southbound rake of coal empties in check as it descends Beattock in summer 1962. When descending long gradients such as Beattock with a train of un-fitted wagons it was often necessary for the guard to pin down half a dozen or so wagon brakes to help the driver keep the train under control.

Right: In August 1961 Fowler LMS 'Patriot' 4-6-0 No 45513, from Carnforth shed, approaches Beattock Summit with the 13-carriage 2pm Manchester Victoria–Glasgow Central express. The appearance of un-rebuilt 'Patriots' north of the border was comparatively rare, and Bill managed to photograph this train in three locations during its ascent of the bank. It had stopped at Beattock to take a banking engine.

Upper left: One of the five 'Rebuilt Royal Scot' 4-6-0s allocated to Polmadie, No 46102 *Black Watch*, with a blue background to its smokebox numberplate, passes Greskine as it climbs Beattock with a northbound express in June 1957.

Lower left: Stanier 'Princess Royal' Pacific No 46210 *Lady Patricia* near Greskine as it climbs Beattock in the early morning with an overnight Euston–Glasgow Central express in July 1958. The second vehicle is a 12-wheel sleeping car. Polmadie had only two of these engines on its allocation at this time.

Right: The first of the 10 'Clan' Pacifics, No 72000 *Clan Buchanan*, from Polmadie shed, makes a fine sight near Harthope as it climbs Beattock with a Manchester/Liverpool–Glasgow/Edinburgh express *c*1956.

72000

Left: The safety valves of an unidentified Fairburn LMS Class 4MT 2-6-4T have lifted as the driver eases for an adverse signal near Greskine on the climb to Beattock with an early-morning pick-up goods that includes the empty carriage for 'The Siege' in August 1963. 'The Siege' was a special train that ran on Saturday mornings for the benefit of the wives and families of railwaymen living in the railway cottages on Beattock Bank and at the summit to allow them to get down to Moffat to do the weekly shopping. Any of the returning bankers would take the coach down to Beattock, and it returned around mid-day.

Right: Named after its designer, the penultimate 'Coronation' Pacific to be built, No 46256 *Sir William A. Stanier, F.R.S.*, climbs Beattock near Harthope with a northbound express in the spring of 1961. Note the modified cab side and trailing truck fitted to this engine and No 46257, completed in 1947/8.

Index of Locations

Index of Locomotive Classes